GW00854492

Basque for Beginners and Novices

by

David S. Luton

Copyright © 2014 David S. Luton

ISBN: 978-1499350883

Table of Contents

Pronunciation

Vowels
a – as in *father*
e – as in *café*
i – as in *police*
o – as in *go*
u – as in *rude*

Diphthongs
ai – like *i* as in *kite*
ei – as in *weigh*
oi – as in *noise*
au – like *ou* as in *house*
eu – like *eh-ooh*, and **not** like *eu* in English

Consonants
Many **consonants** are pronounced more or less like English. Here as some notable differences:

g – always hard as in the word *go*
h – alway silent, excepts in parts of the Basque Country, especially the northern part where it's pronounced like an English h
j – usually like an *h* or a *y* in English in the south, like the *s* in *pleasure* in the north

il – if followed by a vowel like *ly* or *lli* in the word *million*
ñ or *in* followed by a vowel – like *ny* in *canyon*

5

s – similar to *ss* as in *class*, occasionally having almost an *sh* sound with some speakers, **never** having a z sound as in the English word *nose*

z – like *ss* as in *class*, never like an English z

r – very different from an American r, perhaps like the r in the word *very* when pronounced by someone from England; trilled when doubled or before a consonant

x – usually like *sh* in English, occasionally like an s with some words like *taxi*

tx – like *ch* in the word *church*

Ikasgelan
(in the classroom)

nik **daukat** – I have
zuk **daukazu** – you have
hark **dauka** – he/she has
guk **daukagu** – we have
zuek **daukazue** – you all have
haiek **daukate** – they have

nik **behar dut** – I need
zuk **behar duzu** – you need
hark **behar du** – he/she needs
guk **behar dugu** – we need
zuek **behar duzue** – you all need
haiek **behar dute** – they need

liburu bat – a book
boligrafo bat – a pen

In Basque, normally the plural is formed by adding –k or
–ak on the end of a word.

liburu - book
liburuak – books

boligrafo – pen
boligrafoak – pens

arbel – blackboard
aulki – chair, seat
boligrafo/luma – pen
borragoma – rubber (UK)/eraser (US)
esaldi – phrase/sentence
gaia/ikasgaia – lesson
idazmahaia/ikasmahaia – desk
ikasgela – classroom
ikaskide – classmate/class member
kapitulu – chapter
klase – class
koaderno – notebook
konsonantea – consonant
kurtso/ikasturte – course
lapitz/arbatz – pencil
letra/hizkia – letter
liburu – book
mahaia – table
motxila – bookbag, backpack, rucksack
orrialde/orri – page
paper – paper
paragrafo – paragraph

Agurrak
(greetings and farewells)

Kaixo! – Hello!/Hi!
Aupa! – Hi!/Hey! (less formal)

Egun on. – Good morning.
Arratsalde on. – Good afternoon./Good evening.
Arrats on. – Good evening.
Gab on./Gau on. – Good night.

Agur. – Good-bye.
Gero arte. – See you later.
Bihar arte. – See you tomorrow.

Zer moduz?/Zer moduz zaude? – How are you?
Ondo, eta zu? – Fine, and you?
Ondo, eta zuek? – Fine, and you all?

ondo/ongi – good, fine, well
oso ondo/oso ongi– very good/very well
gaizki – bad, not well
oso gaizki – very bad, not very well
izugarri - terrible
hala hola/erdizka – okay/so-so

bai - yes
ez – no (also *not* to form the negative)
agian – maybe/perhaps

Jakina! – Of course!
Atsegin handiz! – Gladly!

Eskerrik asko. – Thank you.
Mila esker. – Thank you very much.
Ez horregatik. – You're welcome.

Mesedez. – Please. (also, "If you don't mind.")

Ongi etorri!/ Ongi etorri (guztiok)! – Welcome!
(singular and plural)

Zorionak! – Congratulations!
Dominu! – Bless you!
Topa! – Cheers!

Barkatu! – Excuse me!/Sorry!
Barkatu, mesedez... – Excuse me, please...

Barkutu! – Hey! (formal)
Aizu! – Hey! (informal, literally *Listen!*)

Badakizu...? – Do you know..?
Badakizu euskaraz? – Do you speak Basque?

Euskalduna zara? – Are you Basque?

Jende eta aurkezpenak
(people and introductions)

...aurkezten dizut. – I'd like you to meet...
...aurkezten dizuet. – I'd like you all to meet...

Hau...da. – This is...
Huaek...dira. – These are...

nire laguna – my friend
nire auzokide – my neighbor
nire lankide – my co-worker
nire lankideak – my co-workers
nire ikaskide– my classmate

nire senarra – my husband/spouse
nire emaztea/andrea – my wife/spouse

nire semea – my son
nire semeak – my sons
nire alaba – my daughter
nire alabak – my daughters
nire seme-alabak – my children

nire aita – my father, dad
nire ama – my mother, mom, mum
nire gurasoak – my parents

nire anaia– my brother
nire neba – my brother (spec. of a female in some parts)

nire arreba– my sister (of a male)
nire ahizpa - my sister (of a female)

nire osaba – my uncle
nire izeba – my aunt

nire aitona – my grandfather
nire amona – my grandmother
nire biloba – my grandson, granddaughter, grandchild
nire bilobak – my grandchildren

nire iloba – my nephew/niece
nire lehengusua – my cousin
nire lehengusuak – my cousins
nire mutil-laguna – my boyfriend
nire neska-laguna – my girlfriend

Zein da zure izena?/Nola duzu izena? – What's your name?
Nire izena...da. – My name is...

Zein da bere izena? – What's his/her name?
Bere izena...da. – His/Her name is...

Zu ezagutzeak pozten nau./Pozten naiz zu ezagutzeaz.
– Nice to meet you.
Berdin. – Likewise.

Lanpostuak, lanbideak eta lanbideei
(jobs, occupations and professions)

Zer egiten duzu? – What do you do (for a living)?
Zein da dure landidea? – What is your occupation?
Ez daukat lanik. – I don't have a job./I'm unemployed.
Irakasle bat naiz. – I am a teacher.

izan (to be)

ni...naiz – I am...
zu...zara – you are...
hura...da – he/she is...

gu...gara – we are...
zuek...zarete – you all are...
haiek...dira – they are...

irakaslea – the teacher
irakasle bat – a teacher
Irakasle bat naiz. – I am a teacher.

aktorea – actor
aktoresa – actress
arkitektua – architect
astronauta – astronaut
abokatua – lawyer
botikaria – pharmacist
enpresaria – businessman/businesswoman
erizaina – nurse
funtzionario – civil servant/government employee

idazkaria – secretary
ikaslea – student
ingeniaria – engineer
irakaslea – teacher
kantaria – singer
kazetaria – journalist
kontablea – accountant
kutxazaina – cashier
medikua – doctor/physician
mekanikari – mechanic
musikaria – musician
nekazaria – farmer
polizia – policeman, policeofficer
zerbitzaria – waiter/waitress

Non egiten duzu lan? – Where do you work?
...lan egiten dut. – I work...
bulego batean – in an office
eskola batean – in a school
fabrika batean – in a factory

Bulego batean lan egiten dut. – I work in an office.

Herrialde eta herriak
(countries and cities)

ni...naiz – I am...
zu...zara – you are...
hura...da – he/she is...
gu...gara – we are...
zuek...zarete – you all are...
haiek...dira – they are...

alemaniako - German
amerikano – American
belgikako – Belgian
eskoses – Scottish
errusiako – Russian
espaniol – Spanish
euskaldun – Basque
frantses – French
gales – Welsh
ingles – English
irlandes – Irish
portugalera – Portuguese
suitzako – Swiss
txinako – Chinese

Euskalduna zara? – Are you Basque?
Ez, irlandesa naiz. – No, Im Irish.

Nongoa zara? – Where are you from?
....*naiz.* – I'm...

Nongoak zarete? – Where are you all from?
Nongoak gara (gu)? – Where are we from?
...*gara.* – We're...

Nongoa da (hura)? – Where's he/she from?
...*da.* – He/She is...

Nongoak dira (haiek)? – Where are they from?
...*dira.* – They're...

Estatu Batuakkoa(k) – from the U.S.
Erresumakoa(k) – from Great Britain.
Ingalaterrakoa(k) – from England
Euskal Herriakoa(k)/Euskadiakoak – from the Basque Country
Eskoziakoa(k) – from Scotland
Galeskoa(k) – from Wales
Irlandakoa(k) – from Ireland
Espainiakoa(k) – from Spain
Frantziakoa(k) – from France
Alemaniakoa(k) – from Germany
Belgikakoa(k) – from Belgium
Suizakoa(k) – from Switzerland
Italiakoa(k) – from Italy
Danimarkakoa(k) – from Denmark

Suezikoa(k) – from Sweden
Greziakoa(k) – from Greece
Egiptokoa(k) – from Egypt
Algeriakoa(k) – from Algeria
Marokokoa(k) – from Morroco

Non bizi zara zu? – Where do you live?
...n bizi naiz. – I live in..

Non bizi da hura? – Where does he/she live?
...n bizi da. – He/She lives in...

Non bizi zarete zuek? – Where do you all live?
...n bizi gara. – We live in...

Non bizi dira haiek? – Where do they live?
...n bizi dira. – They live in...

Berlinen – in Berlin
Bruselan – in Brussels
Erroman – in Rome
Genevan – in Geneva
Lisboan – in Lisbon
Londresen – in London
Munichen – in Munich
Muskuen – in Moscow
Parisen – in Paris
Vienan – in Vienna

Bilboan – in Bilbao
Donostian – in San Sebastian
Iruñean – in Pamplona
Gasteizen – in Vitoria (capital of Spanish Basque Country)

Berlinen bizi naiz. – I live in Berlin.

Adina eta zenbakiak
(age and numbers)

Zenbat urte dituzu zuk? – How old are you?
Nik hamabost urte ditut. – I'm fifteen years old.

Zenbat urte ditu hark? – How old is he/she?
Hark...urte ditu. – He/She is...years old.

Zenbat urte dituzte haiek? – How old are they?
Haiek...urte dituzte. – They're...years old.

Zenbat urte dituzue zuek? – How old are you all?
Guk...urte ditugu. – We're...years old.

bat - 1
bi - 2
hiru - 3
lau - 4
bost - 5
sei - 6
zazpi - 7
zortzi - 8
bederatzi - 9
hamar - 10
hamaika - 11
hamabi - 12
hamahiru - 13
hamalau - 14
hamabost - 15
hamasei - 16

hamazazpi - 17
hamazortzi - 18
hemeretzi - 19
hogei - 20
hogeitabat - 21
hogeitabi – 22, etc.
hogeitahamar - 30
berrogei - 40
berrogeitahamar - 50
hirurogei - 60
hirurogeitahamar - 70
larogei/laurogei - 80
larogeitahamar - 90
ehun - 100
ehunda bat - 101
ehunda bi – 102, etc.

berrehun – 200
hirurehun – 300
laurehun – 400
bostehun – 500
seirehun – 600
zazpirehun – 700
zortzirehun – 800
bederatzirehun – 900

mila – 1,000 (pronounced *milya*)

Jendea eta arropa
(people and clothing)

Nolakoa da hura? – What is he/she like?
Hura...da. – He/She is...

Nolakoak dira haiek? – What are they like?
Haiek...dira. – They're...

altu/handi - tall
baxua/txikia – short

handi/-tzar/-gaitz – big, large
txiki/xume/ttattar – little, small

argala/mehe - thin
gantz - fat

eder(ra)/polit - pretty, attractive, good-looking, beautiful
itsusi - ugly

serio/formal/zintzo - serious
barregarri - funny

interesgarri - interesting
aspergarri - boring

atsegina – nice, pleasant
buruargi/burutsu/argitsu - intelligent

adeitsu/urguri – polite/well-mannered
oihes/zakar – impolite/rude/ill-mannered

on - good
gaizto/txar - bad

langilea – hardworking, industrious
nagi/alfer - lazy

ilehori - blond
beltzaran – dark-haired
ilegorri – red-haired
brontzeztaketa - tanned

nik *daukat* – I have
zuk *daukazu* – you have
hark *dauka* – he/she has

guk *daukagu* – we have
zuek *daukazue* – you all have
haiek *daukate* – they have

ile **luzea** – long hair
ile **motza** – short hair
ile **leuna/liso/zut** – straight hair
ile **kizkurra** – curly hair

ile **beltza** – black hair
ile **marroia** – brown hair
ile **horia** – blond hair
ile **gorria** – red hair

begi **marroiak** – brown eyes
begi **urdinak** – blue eyes
begi **berdeak** – green eyes

janzten dut... – I wear.../I'm wearing...

azpiko arropa/azpiko jantzi - underware
azpiko galtzak/galtzontziloak - underpants
kulotak/kuleroak – panties (US)/knickers (UK)
bularretako – bra

galtzerdiak - socks
zapatak - shoes
botak - boots
zapatilak – sneakers (US)/trainers (UK); slippers

galtzak/praka – pants (US)/trousers (UK)
bakero - jeans
galta motzak - shorts

soineko/janzki – dress, suit
gona – skirt

mediak – pantyhose, nylons (US)/tights (UK)
blusa - blouse

alkondara - shirt
kamiseta – T-shirt
jertse – sweater (US)/jersey, jumper (UK)

kapela - hat
gerriko - belt
gorbata- tie
zapia – handerkerchief, decorative scarf
bufanda – winter scarf, muffler

berokia – coat, overcoat
zira – raincoat, mac
aterki/euritakoa - umbrella

jaka/txamarra - jacket
eskularruak - gloves

janzki/traje - suit
bainujantzia - swimsuit

zorroa/poltsa – handbag (UK)/purse (US)
diru zorro/kartera – wallet/billfold

betaurrekoak - glasses
eguzkitako betaurrekoak – sunglasses

kotoia - cotton
artilea - wool
seta - silk

Koloreak
(colors)

zuria - white
beltza - black

grisa –gray/grey
marroi – brown

gorri - red
larrosa – pink

laranja - orange
horia – yellow

urdina – blue
morea - purple

berdea – green

argia - light
iluna – dark

Egunak, hilabeteak eta data
(days, months and dates)

Ze egun da gaur? – What day is today?
Gaur...da. – Today is...

astelehena - Monday
asteartea - Tuesday
asteazkena - Wednesday
osteguna - Thursday
ostirala - Friday
larunbata - Saturday
igandea – Sunday

urtarrila - January
otzaila - February
martxoa -March
apirila - April
maiatza - May
ekaina - June
uztaila - July
abuztua - August
iraila - September
urria - October
azaroa - November
abendua – December

negua – winter
udaberria - spring
uda - summer
udazkena – autumn/fall

bat - 1
bi - 2
hiru - 3
lau - 4
bost - 5
sei - 6
zazpi - 7
zortzi - 8
bederatzi - 9
hamar - 10
hamaika - 11
hamabi - 12
hamahiru - 13
hamalau - 14
hamabost - 15
hamasei - 16
hamazazpi - 17
hamazortzi - 18
hemeretzi - 19
hogei - 20
hogeita bat - 21
hogeita bi - 22
hogeita hiru – 23, etc.
hogeita hamar - 30
hogeita hamaika - 31

Gaur martxoak 5 da. – Today is March 5th.
2005ko apirilak bi – April 2, 2005

atzo - yesterday
erenegun – the day before yesterday
bihar - tomorrow

aste hau – this week
pasa den astea – last week
hurrengo astea – next week

hilabete hau – this month
pasa den hilabetea – last month
hurrengo hilabetea – next month

urte hau – this year
pasa den urtea – last year
hurrengo urtea – next year

Ordua
(telling time)

Zer ordu da? – What time is it?

Ordu bata da. – It's one o'clock.
Ordu bata eta hamar dira. – It's one ten (1:10)
Ordu bata eta laurden dira. – It's quarter past one. (1:15)
Ordu bat t'erdiak dira. – It's one thirty. (1:30)
Ordu bata hogeita bost gutxi da. – It's twenty five to one. (12:35)

Ordu biak dira. - It's two o'clock.
Hirurak dira. – It's three o'clock.

Hirurak eta hamar dira. – It's three ten. (3:10)
Bostak laurden gutxi dira. – It's a quarter to five. (4:45)
Zortziak dira. – It's eight o'clock.

Hamarrak eta hogeita bost dira. – It's ten twenty five. (10:25)
Hamarrak hamar gutxi dira. – It's ten to ten. (9:50)

goizeko – in the morning
arratsaldeko – in the afternoon
gaueko – in the evening
eguerdia – noon/midday
gauerdia – midnight

Eguraldia
(the weather)

Nolakoa da eguraldia? – How's the weather?

Eguraldi ona dago. – It's nice weather.
Eguraldi txarra dago. – It's bad weather.
Hotz dago. – It's cold.
Fresko dago. – It's cool.
Bero dago. – It's hot.
Eguzkia dago. – It's sunny.
Haizea dago. – It's windy.

Zer egingo du bihar? – What will the weather be like tomorrow?

Hotz egingo du. – It will be cold.
Fresko egingo du. – It will be cool.
Bero egingo du. – It will be hot.
Euria egingo du. – It's going to rain.
Elura egingo du. – It's going to snow.

ekaitz – storm
elur – snow
euri – rain
hodei – cloud
zeru – sky

negu - winter
udaberri - spring
uda - summer
udazken – fall/autumn

Sentimenduak eta baldintzak
(feelings and conditions)

Nola zaude?/Zer moduz zaude? – How are you?
Nola zaudete?/Zer moduz zaudete? – How are you all?

Nola dago?/Zer moduz dago? – How is he/she?
Nola daude?/Zer moduz daude? – How are they?

egon (to be)

ni *nago* – I am
zu *zaude* – you are
hura *dago* – he/she is

gu *gaude* – we are
haiek *daude* – they are
zuek *zaudete* – you all are

pozik – happy, content
triste – sad
triste/ilun/malerus – unhappy

hunkituta/bero-bero – excited
deprimitu – depressed
dezepzionatu – dissappointed/let down

lasai – calm
urduri – nervous
ketkaturik – worried

okupatuta – busy
haserretuta – angry
iraulketa/iraultze – upset

eroa – crazy
zentzudun – sane

gaixorik/zorigaitz – ill
nekatuta – tired

Gorputza
(the body)

buru - head
bekoki/kopeta/betondo - forehead
burezur/garezur - skull
burmuin/zerebro - brain
ile - hair
belarri – ear

aurpegi - face
begi - eye
bekain/bepuru - eyebrow
betile - eyelash
masail/matela - cheek
sudur - nose

aho - mouth
ezpain/musu - lip
mihi/mingain - tongue
hortz - tooth

kokots/okotz/bidar – chin
lepo – neck
eztarri/zintzur - throat
bizkar - back

beso – arm
sorbalda/besaburu - shoulder
ukondo/ukalondo - elbow
eskutur - wrist

esku - hand
hatz/atzamar/eri - finger
azazkal - fingernail

bular – chest, breast
bihotz - heart
birika - lung
gibel - liver
giltzurrun - kidney
urdail - stomach

hanka - leg
izter - thigh
belaun - knee
oin - foot
orkatila - ankle
orpo - heel
oinazpi - sole

azal - skin
odol – blood

Jarduera eta lekuak
(activities and places)

...gustatzen... (to like)

zait/zaizkit – I like
zaizu/zaizkizu – you like
zaio/zaizkio – he/she likes
zaigu/zaizkigu – we like
zaizue/zaizkizue – you all like
zaie/zaizkie – they like

For example:

Gustatzen zait... – I like...
Asko gustatzen zait... – I really like....

Asko gustatzen zait zinemara joatea. – I really like to go to the cinema.

kanpatu/etxolatu – to camp
datzatu – to dance
kantu – to sing
korrika egin/kurritu – to run
irakurri/leitu – to read
marraztu/diseinatu – to draw
jokatu (kirol) – to play sports
jo/jotzen (musika) – to play music
ostera egin/paseatu – to go for a walk/stroll
hitz egin – to speak/talk
musika entzun – to listen to music

pintatu – to paint
bide egin/ibili – to walk
labain egin – to skate

Ni...noa. – I'm going...
Zu...zoaz. – You're going...
Hura...doa. – He/She is going...
Gu...goaz. – We're going...
Zuek... zoazte. – You all are going...
Haiek...doaz. – They're going...

ardotegiara – to the wine shop
arraindegiara – to the fish shop/fishmonger's
azokara – to the market
burdindegiara – to the hardware store/ironmonger's
elizara – to the church
enparantzara – to the (town) square
etxera – (to) home
farmaziara – to the pharmacy/chemist's
gasolindegiara – to the gas/petrol station
geltokiara – to the station
gozotegiara – to the candy store/sweet shop
haragitegiara – to the butcher's
herriara – to the town, village
hondartzara – to the beach
hotelera – to the hotel
ibaiara – to the river
igerilekuara – to the swimming pool

ileapaindegira – to the hairdresser's
irteera – to the exit, way out
itsasaldera – to the coast
itsasora – to the sea
izozkitegiara – to the icecream parlor/shop
jatetxera – to the restaurant
komisaldegiara – to the police station
kutxara – to the bank
lanera – to work
liburudendara – to the bookshop
mendiara – to the mountains
museora – to the museum
okindegiara – to the baker's
parkera – to the park
portuara – to the port, harbor
sarrera – to the entrance
supermerkatura – to the supermarket
tabernara – to the tavern, pub
tobakoakera – to the tobacconist
udaletxera – to the town hall
zapategiara – to the shoe shop
zineara – to the cinema/movie theater
zubiara – to the bridge

Janaria eta edaria
(food and drinks)

gosari - breakfast
zereal – ceral
ogi – bread
topa – toast
gurin - butter
marmelada – jam
ezti – honey
jogurt – yogurt

bazkaria - lunch
sandwich/otarteko - sandwich
entsalada/gatzozpin - salad
zopa - soup
hanburgesa - hamburger
gazta - cheese
patata – potato
afari – dinner/supper

edariak - drinks
ur - water
zuku/zumo - juice
esne - milk
kafe - coffee
kafesne – coffee with milk
te - tea
garagardo - beer
ardo - wine
ron - rum

mahaia - the table
aizto/kutxilo - knife
sardexka - fork
zali - spoon
mahai-zapi/dafaila - napkin
plater - plate
kikara/xikara - cup
edontzi/vaso - glass
gatz - salt
piper - pepper
azukre - sugar

fruita
sagar - apple
banana/platano - banana
gerezi - cherry
piku - fig
mahats - grape
limoi/zitroi - lemon
meloi – melon/cantaloupe
laranja - orange
melokotoi - peach
madari - pear
anana - pineapple
aran - plum
magurdi - raspberry
marrubi - strawberry
angurri/sandia – watermelon

landare/barazki - vegetables
azaburu - cabbage
azalore - cauliflower
arto – corn/maize
luzkar/pepino - cucumber
berenjena – eggplant (US)/aubergine (UK)
baratxuri - garlic
uraza/letxuga - lettuce
barrengorri - mushroom
oliba - olive
tipula - onion
ilar - pea
espinaka - spinach
tomate – tomato

haragi - meats
behikia - beef
oilasko - chicken
ahate/paita – duck
bildoski - lamb
gibel - liver
txerri – pork
urdaiazpiko - ham
saltxitxa – sausage
indioilar – turkey

itsaski - seafood
antxoa - anchovy
txirla - clam
bakailao - cod
karramarro - crab
arrain - fish
lengoradu – sole/flounder
otorrain - lobster
ostra - oyster
izokin - salmon
izkira - shrimp
txibia - squid
amuarrain - trout
atun – tuna

postre - dessert
txocolate - chocolate
tarta - cake
gaileta – cookie (US)/biscuit (UK)
helatu/izozki – icecream

Miscellaneous
arbendol/almendra - almond
arrautza - eggs
arroz/arris - rice
kakahuete - peanut
inxtaur – walnut, nut
olio - oil

<u>sukaldean - in the kitchen</u>
labe - oven
lata/latontzi – can/tin
lata-irekitzeko – can-opener
botila/bonbil - bottle
kortxo-irekigailu - corkscrew
kopakada - goblet
xanpain - champagne
eltze/lapiko - pot
kokel - saucepan
zartagina – frying pan
erratz - broom
balde/ontzi/pertz - bucket
trapu – dishrag

Norabideak eskatu
(asking for directions)

Barkatu? – Excuse me...
Aizu... – Say..../Excuse me... (less formal)

Non dago...? – Where is...?
Nola joaten da...? – How do you get to...?

Galduta nago. – I'm lost.
Galduta gaude. – We're lost.

Dakit... – I know...
Ez dakit... – I don't know...

Segi... – Continue...

aurrera – forward, ahead
Segi aurrera... – Keep straight.../Keep going straight...

Pasatu...– Pass.../Go past...

eskubi/eskubitara - right
eskubi aldean – on the right(hand side)

esker/eskerretara - left
esker aldean – on the left(hand side)

lehenengo kalea(n) – (on) the first street

aurrean – in front, opposite
ondoan – next to
gertu - near
urruti – far
Dago urruti. – It's far.
Ez dago urruti.* – It's not far.
Ikusiko duzu... – You'll see...
autobia/autopista – highway, motorway
irteera - exit
kalea – street
karretera/errepidea – road
geltokia - station
mapa – map
peaje – toll, toll station, toll booth
plaza/enparantza - square
semafora – traffic light(s)
izkina(n) – (on) the corner

Modes of Transport
abioi/hegazkin – plane
auto/kotxe – car, automobile
autobusa – bus
bizikleta – bicycle, bike
lurpekoa – underground (UK)/subway (US)
moto – motorcycle, motorbike
taxi – taxi (pronounced *tah-si*)
trena – train

Etxean
(at home)

argia - light
armario – closet (US)/wardrobe (UK); cupboard
atea - door
aulkia – chair
bainugela – bathroom
berogailu – heater
buzoi – letterbox, mailbox
egongela/sala – living room
eskailera – stairs, staircase, stairway
etxe – home, house, apartment, flat
gela – room
giltza – key
igogailu – elevator (US)/lift (UK)
irratia - radio
jangela – dining room
kalefazio - heating
komuna – toilet
lanpara - lamp
leihoa – window
logela - bedroom
mahaia - table
ohe – bed
pisu – flat, apartment, floor, storey
sofa – sofa, couch
sukalde - kitchen
telebista – television
telefono – telephone
terraza – balcony/terrace

Animaliak eta natura
(animals and nature)

<u>Animaliak</u>
ahuntza – goat
ardia – sheep
arraina – fish
balea – whale
behia – cow
dortoka – turtle
elefantea – elephant
erlea – bee
hegazta – duck
igela – frog
indioilara – turkey
inurria – ant
jirafa – giraffe
katua – cat
lehoia – lion
oiloa – chicken
sugea – snake
tigrea – tiger
txoria – bird
zakura – dog
zaldia – horse
zezena – bull

<u>Natura</u>
aldapa – hill, slope
arbola – tree
belara – grass
bidea – path
eguzkia - sun
erreka – stream
hondara/harea – sand
hondartza – beach
hostoa/orria – leaf
ibaia – river
itsaso - sea
itsasaldea – coast
lakua – lake
lorea - flower
mendia(k) – mountain(s)
olatua – wave

Gramatika
(basic grammar)

Personal Pronouns

Personal pronouns (i.e. subject pronouns) in Basque are **optional** which means that they are often omitted in situations where they are not needed for emphasis or clarity. They are as follows:

1. **ni** (I)
2. **hi** (you – singular familiar)
Apparently this pronoun is not used in some if not many Basque-speaking areas in favor of *zu* which serves as the formal singular in the areas that *do* use *hi* as the familiar singular. In this book, I will use only *zu* to refer to you singular with no regard to familiar or formal.
3. **zu** (you – singular or singular formal)
This pronoun would translate *you singular* in most Basque-speaking areas, although some which make as distinction between singular familiar and singular formal use *zu* as the formal and *hi* as the familar).

This pronoun is technically plural because apparently it originally served as both the plural and formal singular (like *vous* in French and *Sie* in German). However, in time a new plural was created (zuek) which relegated *zu* to singular formal status.

4. **hura** – also sometimes *bera* (he/she/it)
It seems that Basque doesn't have separate words to represent *he*, *she* and *it* like we do in English. This likely isn't a problem in situations where there is no doubt concerning who or what the subject is. In other situations, one would likely have to clarify by stating someone's name or giving other descriptive words to avoid confusion.

5. **gu** (we)

6. **zuek** (you plural)

7. **haiek/horiek** (they)

Nouns, Adjectives and Articles

In Basque, most nouns have a basic form (a form without suffixes).

The article is normally expressed with the suffix **–a** which would roughly translate *a* or *the* in English; however it is not used in some instances (for example before the number one). Also some words words end with an **–a** in their basic form (e.g. *denda* which means store or shop). For example:

kale – street (basic form)
kalea – a street/the street

denda – store/a store/the store (basic form already ends with **–a**)

In this book, I have often listed vocabulary words using the form that ends with **–a**.

The plural is normally formed by adding the suffix **–k** or **–ak.** When a noun is modified by an adjective, the plural ending goes on the end of the adjective, not on the end of the noun (completely the opposite of English!)

Also notice that the adjective typically comes after the noun (also the opposite of English).
For example:

liburu – book (basic form)
liburua – a book/the book
liburu bat – one book/a book
liburuak – (the) books
liburu handiak –(the) large books

The article is also not used with demonstratives like *hau* (this). For example:

Liburu hau handi da. – This book is big.

Prepositions

Prepositions in Basque, like the article, are usually expressed by adding a suffix to a word. For example:

–ekin/–arekin = with/with the
nire aita – my father
nire aitekin – with my father

–n/–en = in, at or on
ikasgela – the classroom
ikasgelan – in the classroom

Londres – London
Londresen – in London

–ra/–era = to
denda – store/shop
dendara – to the shop

–ik = from (the opposite of *to*)
etxe – home
etxetik – from home

–koa = from, a native of
Espainia – Spain
Espainiakoa – from Spain/a native of Spain

Demonstratives
hemen – here
hau – this
hauek - these
hor – there
hori – that
horiek - those
han – over there
hura – that (over there)
haiek – those (over there)

Conjunctions, Connectives, Adverbs
ba– - if (e.g. *badago* = if there is...)
baina – but
bakarrik – only
berriro - again
beti - always
bitartean – meanwhile, in the meantime
edo - or
ere – too, also
eta – and (often pronounced *ta*)
gainera – furthermore, and also
gero – afterwards, later, then
igual – perhaps
orduan - then
orain – now
orainxte – right now
oraindik – still, yet

gaur – today
bihar – tomorrow
laister - soon

Question Words and Phrases
nola? – how?
nolako? – what kind (of)?
non? – where?
nongoa? – from where?/where...from? (place of origin)
nondik? – from where?/where...from? (opposite of *to where?*)
nora? – to where?/where...to?
nor? – who?
noiz – when?
zenbat? – how much?/how many?
zein – which?
zer? – what?
zergakit? – why?

Words of Amount/Quantity
batzuk – some
pare bat – a couple (of)
asko – a lot, much
gutxi – few, little
gehiago – more
gutxiago – less, fewer
dena – all, everything
denak – everyone

Talking about Possession

ni - I
nire/nere – my
niretzat/neretzat – for me

zu - you
zure – your
zuretzat – for you

hura/bera – he/she/it
bere – his/her/its
beretzat – for him/for her/for it

gu – we
gure – our
guretzat – for us

zuek – you all
zuen – your
zuentzat – for you all

haiek/horiek – they
haien/horien/beren – their
haientzat/horientzat – for them

The Verb *to be* in Basque

In Basque there are two verbs which we would both translate *to be* in English (*izan* and *egon*). The latter is used more to describe location or a temporary state:

izan
ni *naiz* – I am
zu *zara* – you are
hura *da* – he/she is

gu *gara* – we are
zuek *zarete* – you all are
haiek *dira* – they are

egon (location or condition)
ni *nago* – I am
zu *zaude* – you are
hura *dago* – he/she is

gu *gaude* – we are
zuek *zaudete* – you all are
haiek *daude* – they are

The verb *bizi* (to live) is formed using *izan*:

ni **bizi** *naiz* – I live
zu **bizi** *zara* – you live
hura **bizi** *da* – he/she lives
gu **bizi** *gara* – we live
zuek **bizi** *zarete* – you all live
haiek **bizi** *dira* – they live

The verb *izan* is also used to form the present continuous (present progressive) in conjunction with the verb form *ari*. For example:

ikasten – to learn
ikasten ari *naiz* – I'm learning
ikasten ari *zara* – you're learning
ikasten ari *da* – he/she is learning
ikasten ari *gara* – we're learning
ikasten ari *zarete* – you all are learning
ikasten ari *dira* – they're learning

We previously saw the verb *behar* (to need) on page 7:

nik behar *dut* – I need
zuk behar *duzu* – you need
hark behar *du* – he/she needs
guk behar *dugu* – we need
zuek behar *duzue* – you all need
haiek behar *dute* – they need

To verb *nahi* (to want) also uses the same forms (*dut*, *duzu*, *du*, *dugu*, *duzue* and *dute*):

nik nahi *dut* – I want
zuk nahi *duzu* – you want
hark nahi *du* – he/she wants
guk nahi *dugu* – we want
zuek nahi *duzue* – you all want
haiek nahi *dute* – they want

66

Other Important Words

Here are some other important words which are in alphabetical order in English and then following in Basque. These are words which haven't appeared in other parts of the book. If you are looking for a word that you don't find here, look for it by topic in the corresponding chapter.

English/Basque
a little – pixka bat
above – goian
after /afterwards– ondoren, gero, eta gero
ago – duela
almost – ia
another – beste…bat
answer – eranztun
anyone – inor
anything – ezer
appear – agertu
around – inguruan
arrive – iritsi
ask – galdetu
ask for – eskatu

Basque Country - Euskadi
Basque language – euskara
Basque speaker – euskaldun
before – baino lehen
behind - atzean

better – hobe, hobeto
bill (in a restaurant) - kontu
both – biak
bring – ekarri
bring out - atera
buy – erosi

call – deitu
cannot – ezin
card – txartel
Careful! – Kontuz!
carry – eraman
catch – harrapatu
change – aldatu
charge – kobratu
cheap – merke
check (in a restaurant) – kontu
clean – garbi
climb - igo
come – etorri
continue – jarraitu, segi
country (nation) – herri

delicious – goxo
dictionary – hiztegi
different – desberdin
difficult – zail
down – behera

each – bakoitz(a)
east – ekialde
easy – erraz
eat – jan
enough – nahiko(a)
especially – batez ere
et cetera – eta abar
exam – azterketa
exchange – aldatu
exchange rate – kanbio
expensive – garesti

famous – ospetsu
fill – bete
find – aurkitu
finish - bukatu

hard (difficult) – zail

I can't – ezin dut
I'd like – nahi nuke
I don't mind – berdin zait
I must/I need (to) – behar dut
inexpensive – merke
information – informazio
inside – barruan
international – nazioarteko

late – berandu
later – gero, beranduago
life – bizitza
like that – horrela(ko)
listen – entzun
look – begiratu
look for – bilatu
lose – galdu

make – egin
menu – karta
morning - goiz

nation – herri
new – berri
news – berriak
newspaper – egunkari
night – gau
north – iparralde

of course – noski
offer – eskaini
old – zahar
on top of – gainean
once – behin
open – irekita
organize – antolatu
out – kanpora

outside – kanpoan
pain – min
pay - ordaindu
party (gathering/celebration) – jai
person – pertsona
peseta (previous Spanish currency) – pezeta
postcard – postal
pound – libra
prepare – prestatu
price – prezio
probably – seguraski
problem – problema
put – ipini, jarri
put in – sartu

quick – azkar
quiet – lasai

ready – prest
really – benetan
region – eskualde
remember – gogoratu
return – itzuli

same – berdin
say – esan
see – ikusi
sell – saldu

send – bidali
show – erakutsi
side – alde
similar – berdin
sit – eseri
sleep – lo egin
song – kanta, abesti
south – hegoalde
special – berezi
start – hasi
stay – gelditu
suitcase – maleta

take – hartu, eraman
take away – kendu
talk – hitzegin
tell – esan
temperature – tenperatura
thing – gauza
ticket – txartel, bilete
time – denbora
together – elkarrekin
too much/too many – gehiegi
town – herri
true – egia
try – saiatu

under – azpian

understand – ulertu
until – arte
up – gora
use – erabili

wait – itxoin
watch (wristwatch) – erloju
way (manner) – modu
way (route) – bide
weekend – asteburu
west – mendebalde
wide – zabal
without – gabe
word – hitz
work – lan (noun); lan egin (verb)
write – idatzi

yet - oraindik
young - gazte

Basque/English

agertu - appear
aldatu - change
aldatu - exchange
alde - side
antolatu - organize
arte - until
asteburu - weekend
atera – bring out
atzean - behind
aurkitu - find
azkar - quick
azpian - under
azterketa - exam

bakoitz(a) - each
baino lehen - before
barruan - inside
batezere - especially
begiratu - look
behar dut – I must/I need (to)
behera - down
behin - once
benetan - really
berandu - late
berdin – same, similar
berdin zait – I don't mind
berezi - special
berri - new

berriak - news
beste...bat - another
bete – fill
biak - both
bidali - bidali
bide – way (route)
bilatu – look for
bizitza - life
bukatu - finish

deitu - call
denbora - time
desberdin - different
duela - ago

egia - true
egin - make
egunkari - newspaper
ekarri - bring
ekialde - east
elkarrekin - together
cntzun - listen
erakutsi - show
eraman - carry
eranztun - answer
erabili - use
erloju - wristwatch
erosi - buy

erraz - easy
esan – say, tell
eseri - sit
eskaini - offer
eskatu – ask for
eskualde - region
eta – and
eta abar – etc.
etorri - come
Euskadi – the Basque Country
euskara – the Basque language (also *euskera*)
euskaldun – a Basque speaker
ezer – anything
 ezin – cannot, can't
ezin dut – I can't

gabe – without
galdetu - ask
galdu - lose
gainean – on top of
garbi - clean
garesti - expensive
gau - night
gauza - thing
gazte - young
gehiegi – too much/too many
gelditu – stay
gero - more

geroago, beranduago - later
gogoratu - remember
goian - above
goiz - morning
gora - up
goxo - delicious
harrapatu - catch
hartu, eraman - take
hasi - start
hegoalde - south
herri – country, nation, town
hitz - word
hitzegi - dictionary
hitzegin - talk
hobe, hobeto - better
horrela(ko) – like that

ia - almost
idatzi - write
igo - climb
ikusi - see
informazio - information
inor - anyone
inguruan - around
iparralde - north
ipini, jarri - put
irekita - open
iritsi - arrive

itxoin - wait
itzuli - return

jai – party (gathering/celebration)
jan - eat
jarraitu, segi - continue

kanbio – exchange rate
kanpoan - outside
kanpora - out
kanta, abesti - song
karta - menu
kendu – remove, take away
kobratu - charge
kontu – bill/check (in a restaurant)
Kontuz! – Careful!

lan – work/job (noun)
lan egin – work (verb)
quiet – lasai - quiet
libra – pound (unit of weight/money)
lo – sleep (noun)
lo egin – sleep (verb)

maleta - suitcase
mendebalde - west
merke – cheap, inexpensive
min - pain

modu – way (manner)

nahiko(a) - enough
nahi nuke – I'd like
nazioarteko - international
noski – of course

ondoren, gero, eta gero – after, afterwards
oraindik - yet
ordaindu - pay
ospetsu - famous

pertsona - person
pixka bat – a little
postal - postcard
prest - ready
prestatu - prepare
prezio - price
problema - problem

saiatu - try
saldu - sell
sartu – put in
seguraski - probably

tenperatura - temperature
txartel, bilete - ticket
txartel - card

ulertu - understand
zabal - wide
zahar - old
zail - difficult

11636608R00051

Printed in Great Britain
by Amazon.co.uk, Ltd.,
Marston Gate.